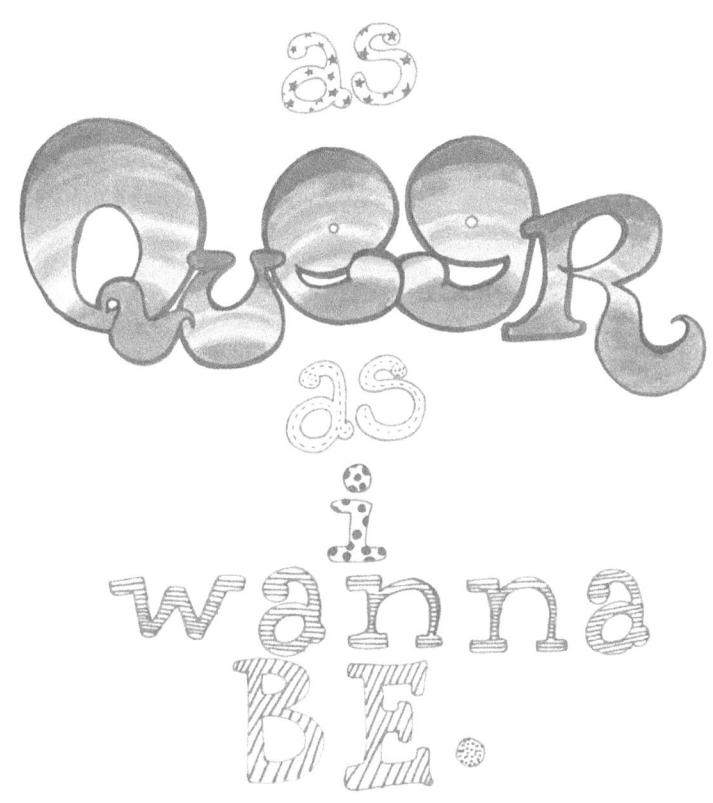

coloring book
illustrated by sam kirk & jenny Q.

we created this book because...

we wanted to.

(...and also because representation
matters, pride for our capacity to love as much as
we do is important to share with the world, and freedom
of expression is paramount... etc. etc.)

- The Quirks

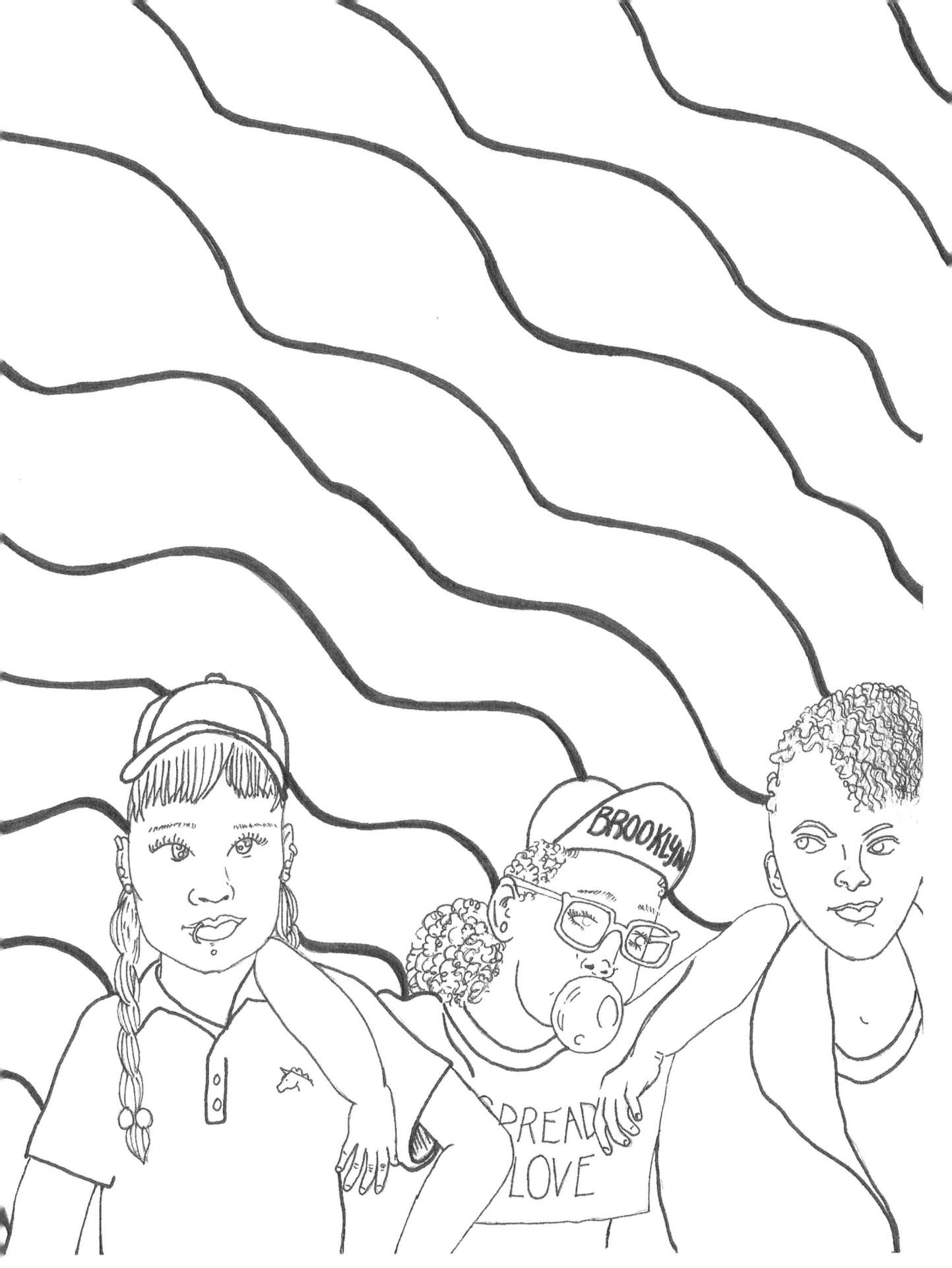

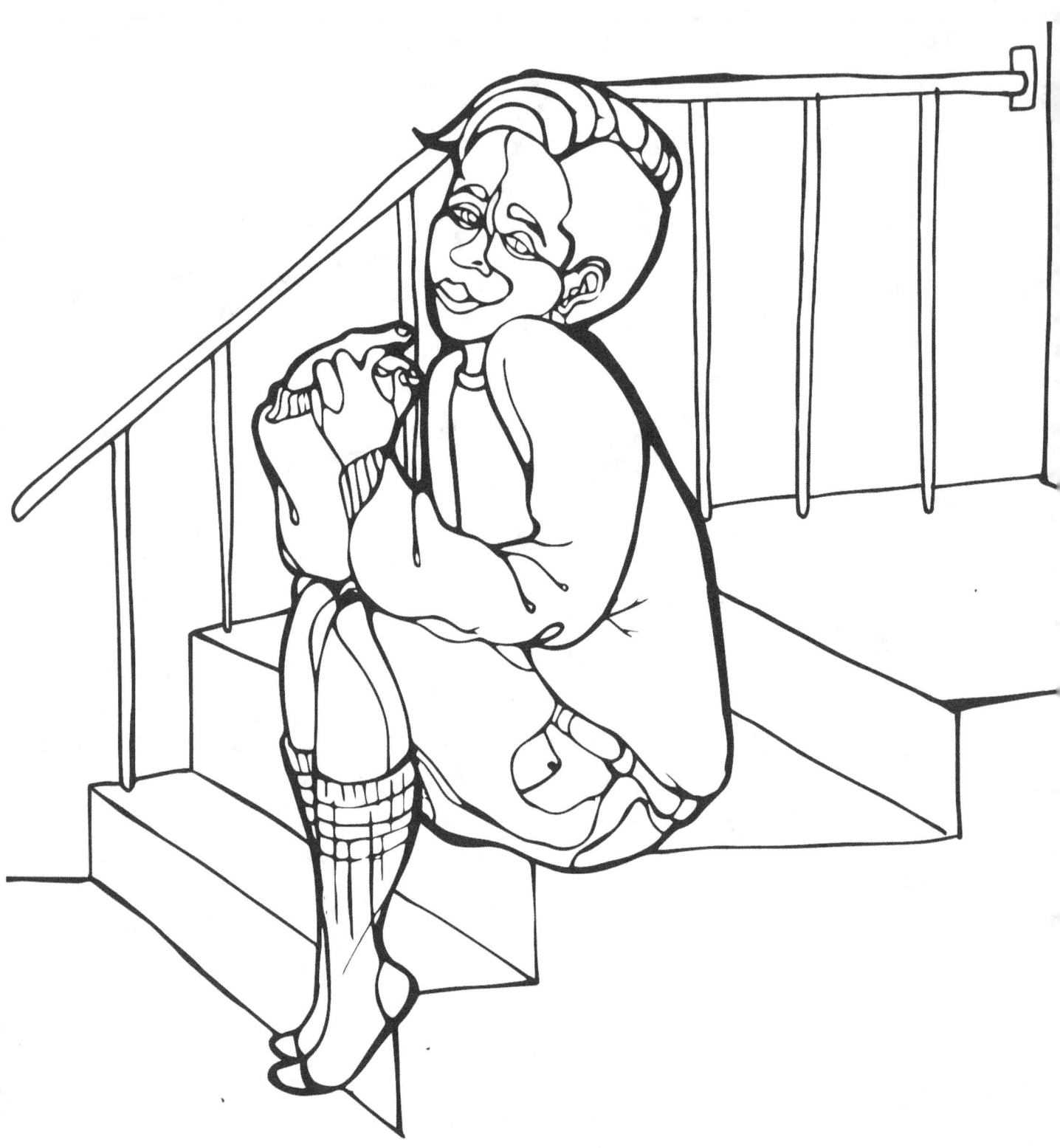

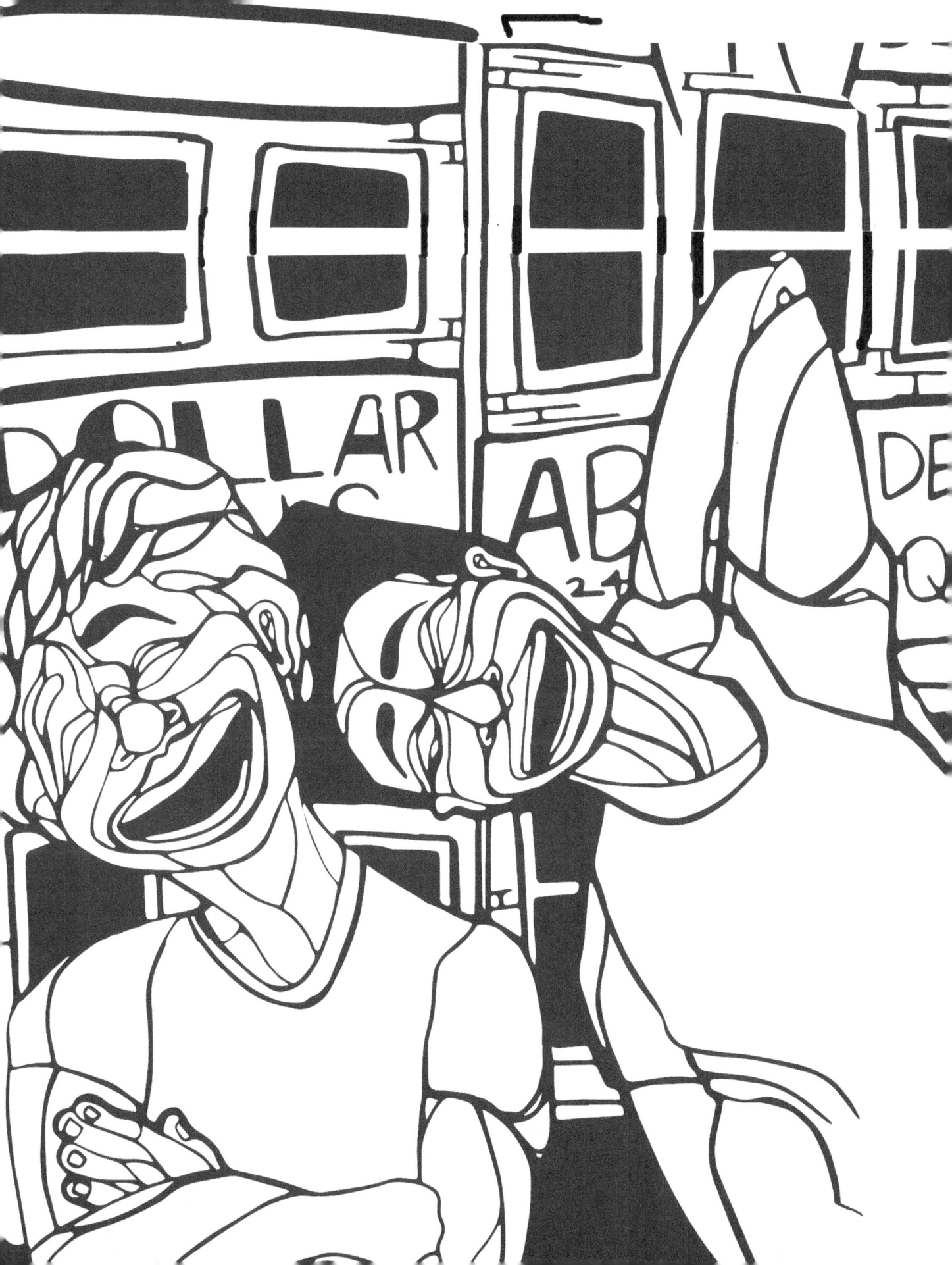

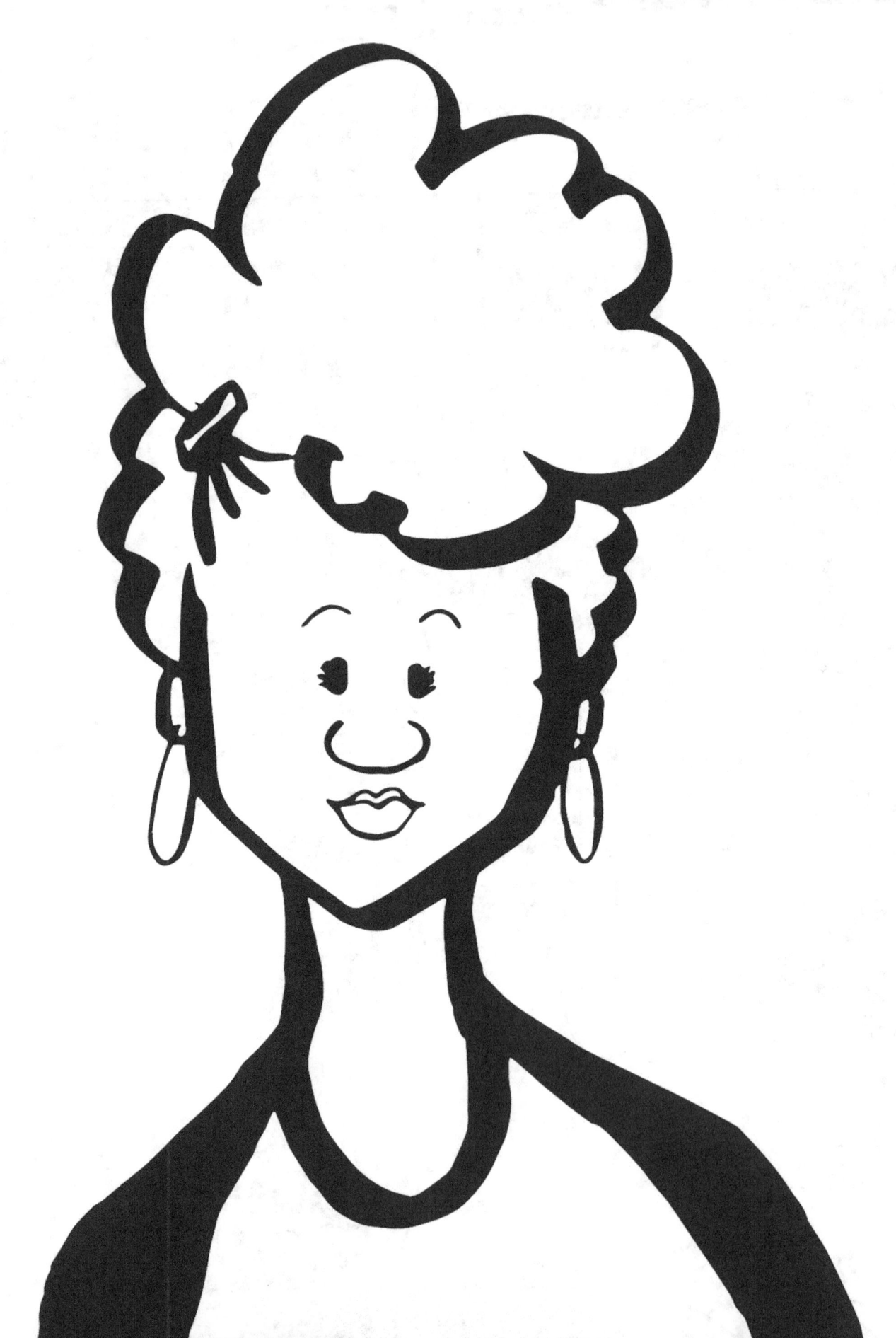

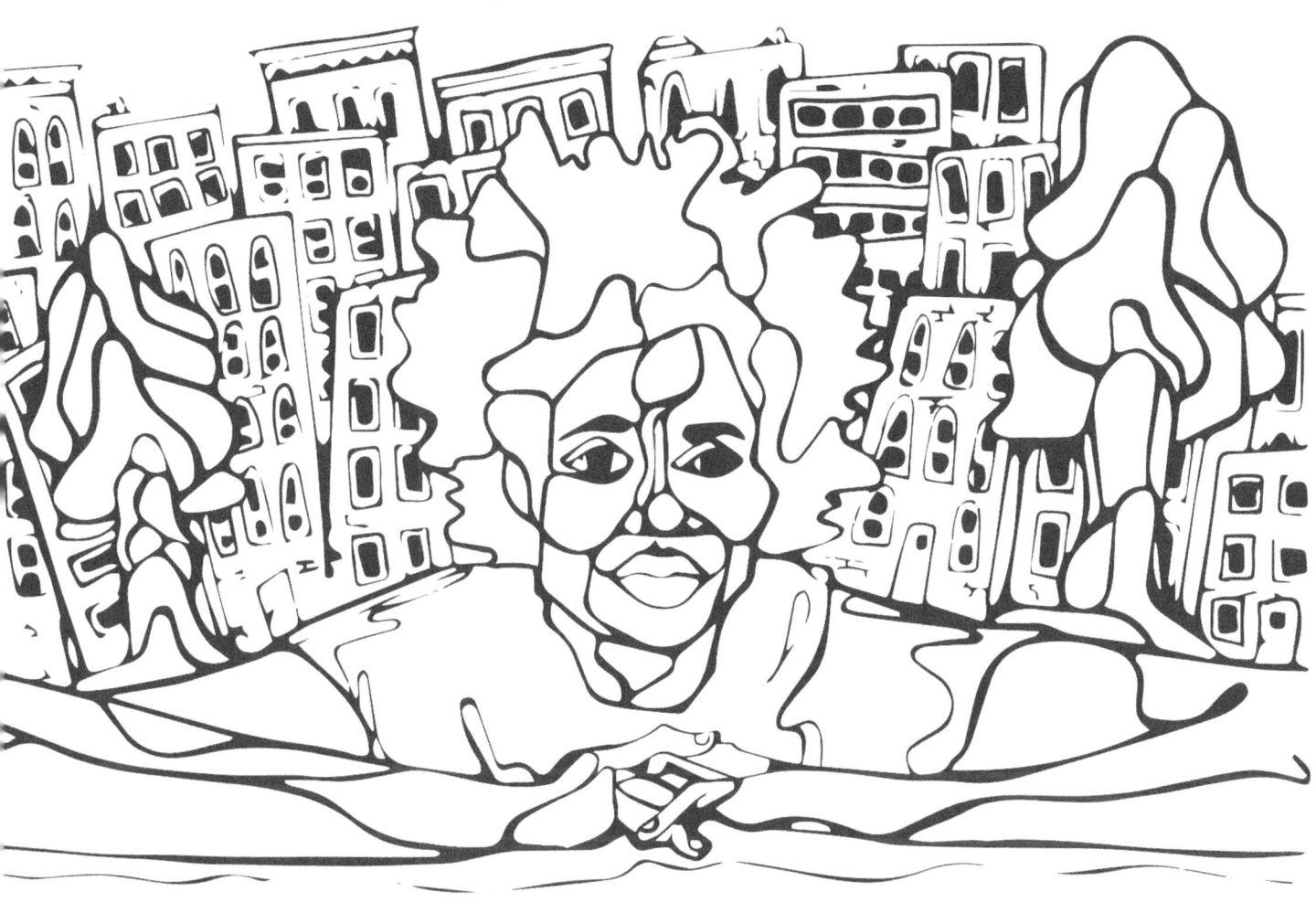

RESPECTFUL   CARE   VALUED

GOALS   KNOWLEDGE

DIGNITY   HEALTHY   HOME

LOVE   EDUCATED

STRENGTH   PRIDE   HONOR

ACCEPTANCE   EQUALITY

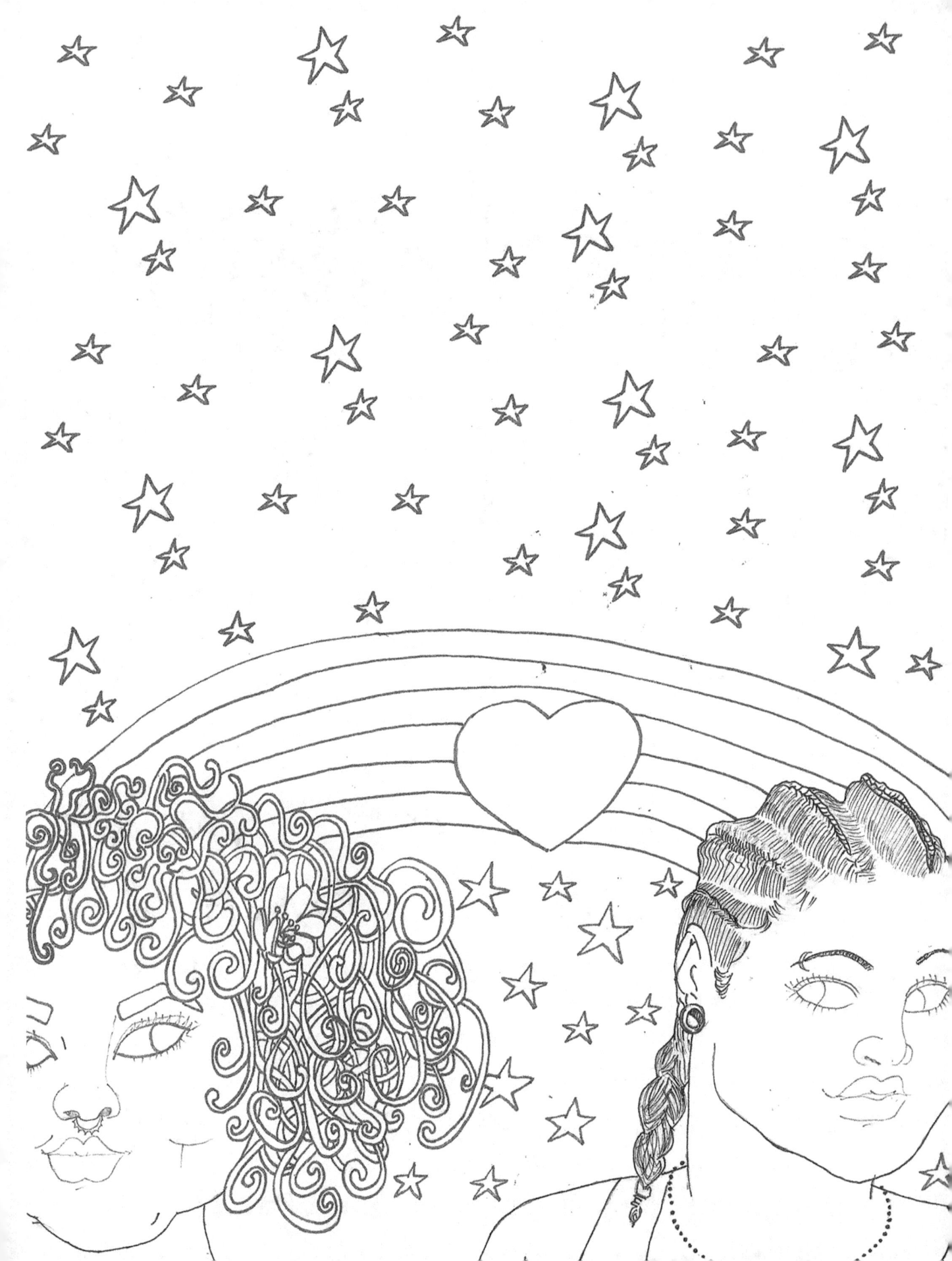

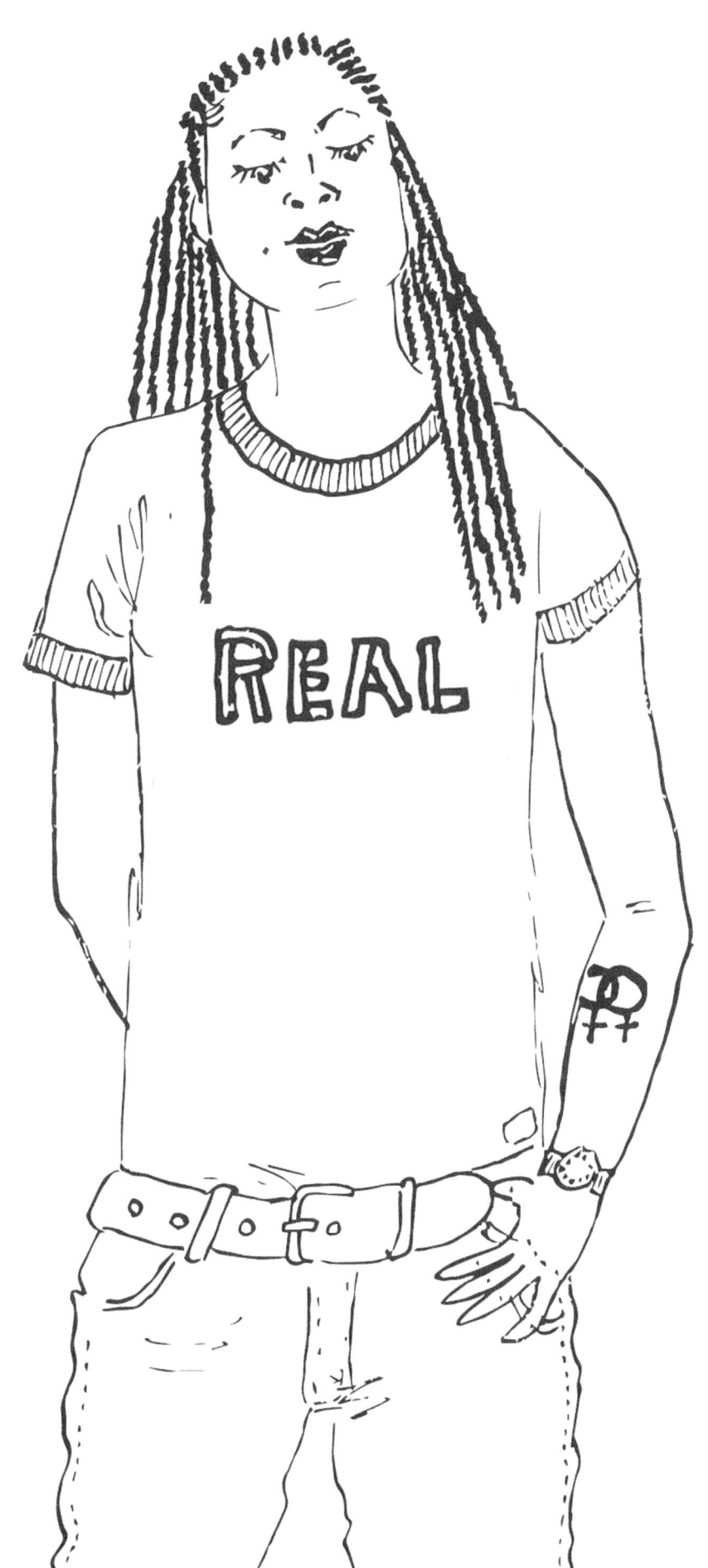

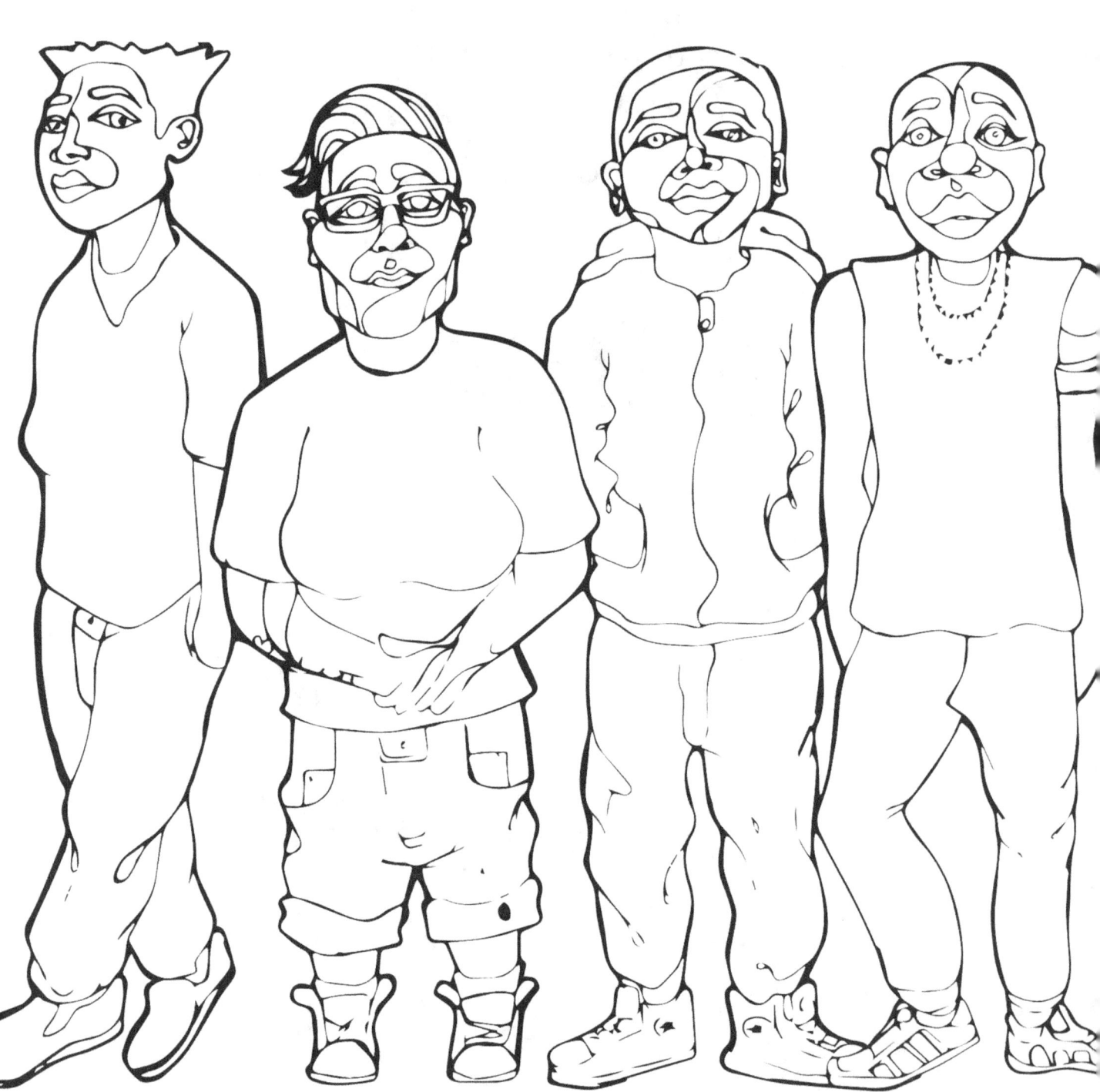

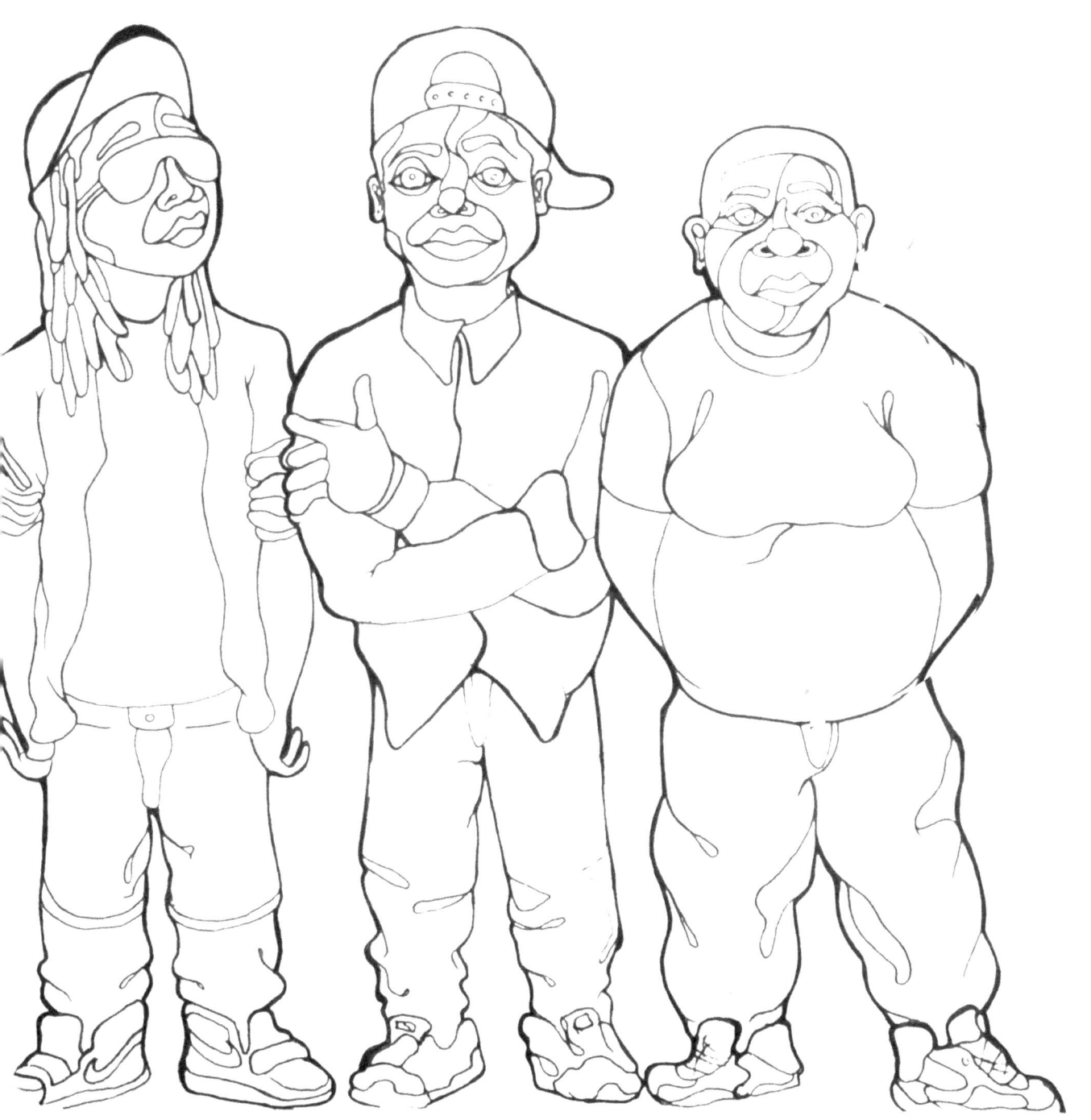

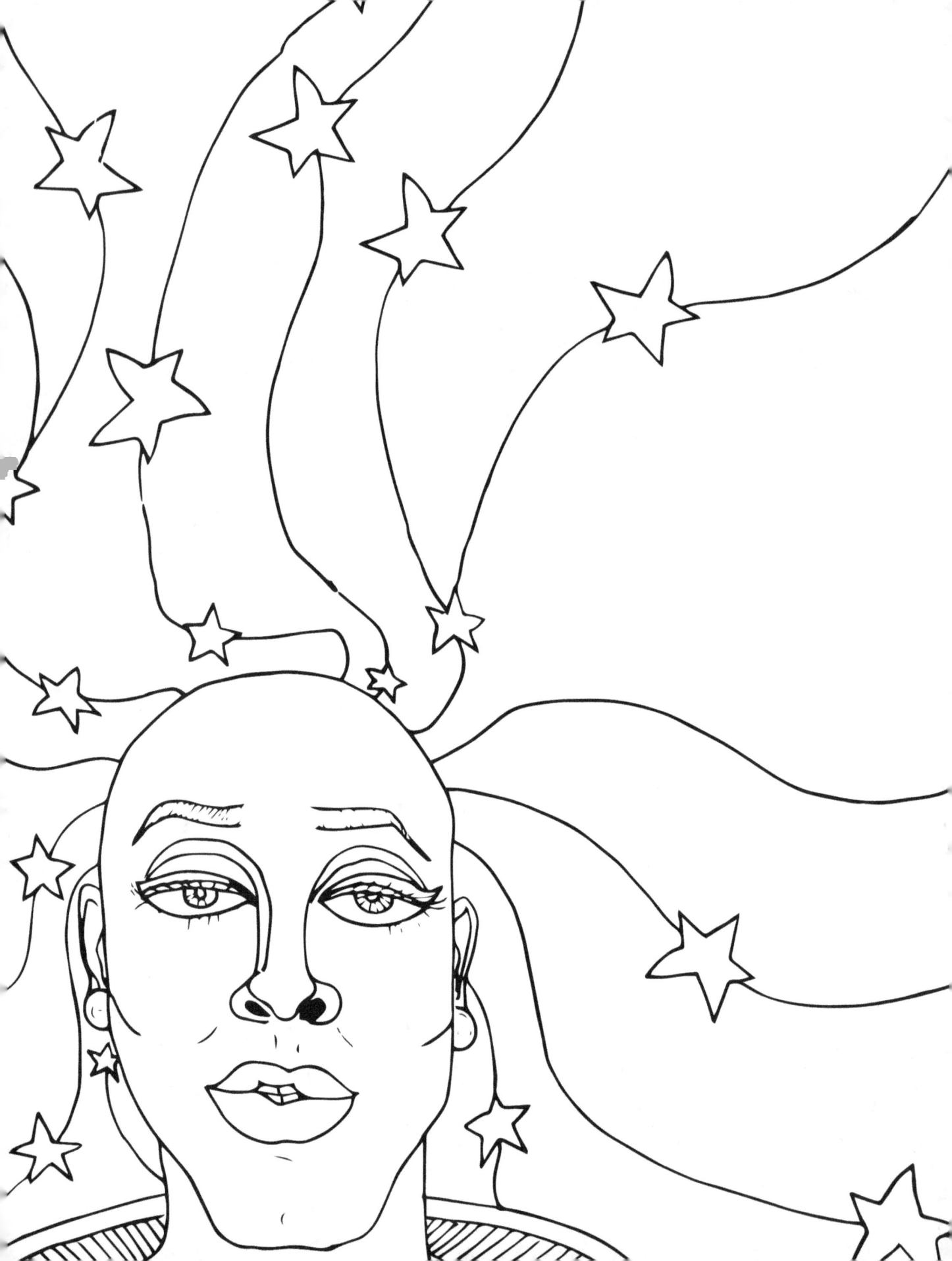

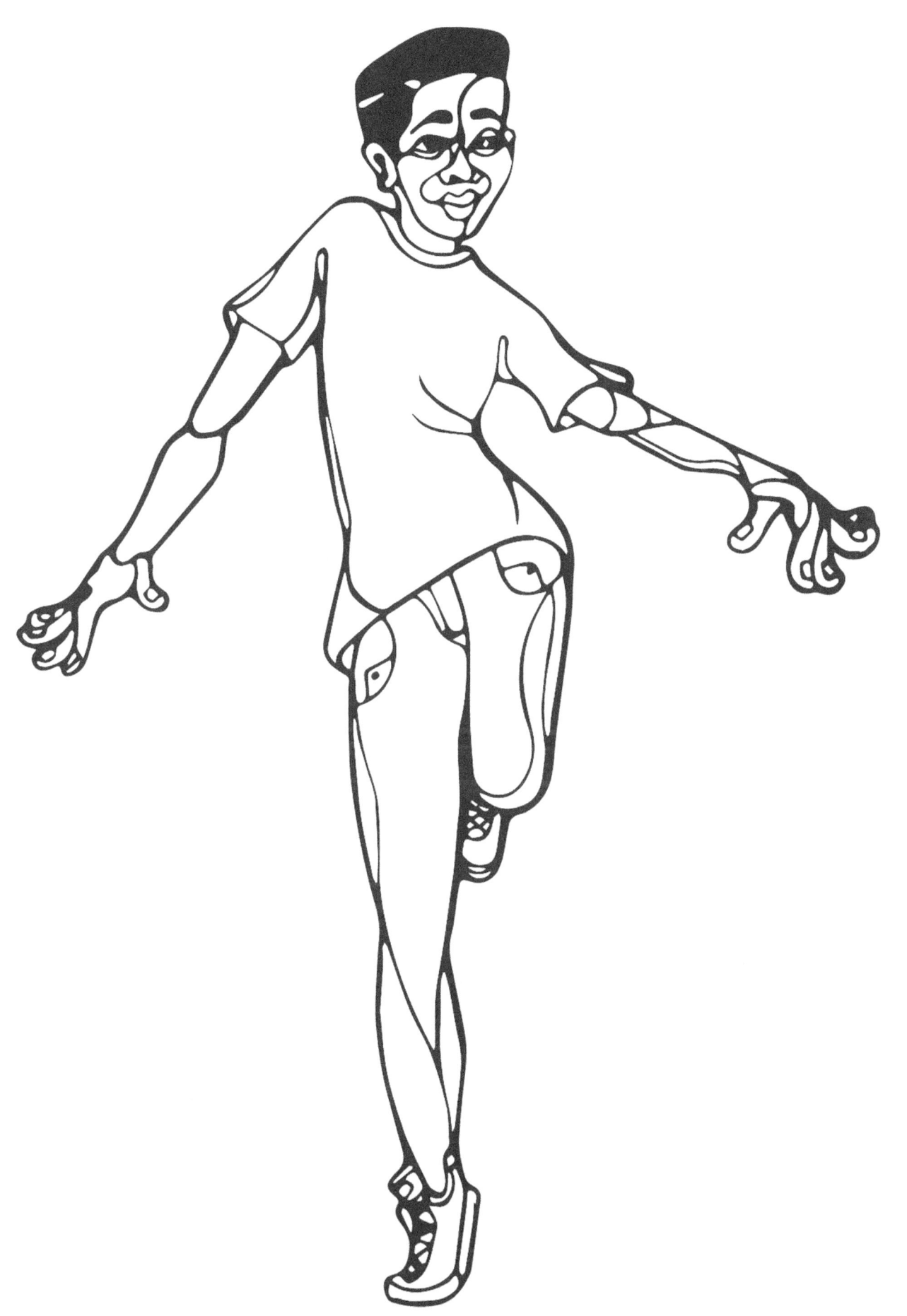

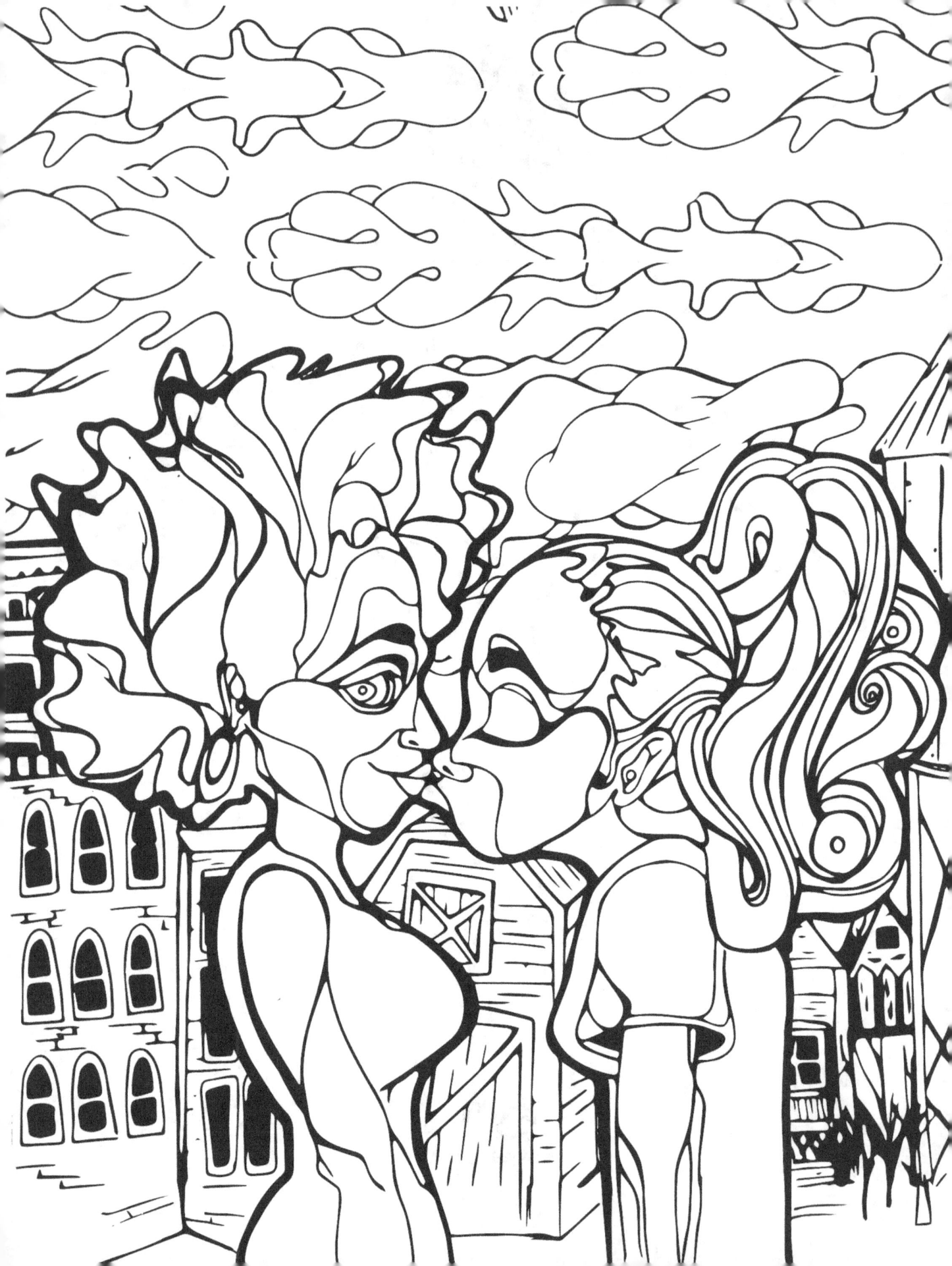

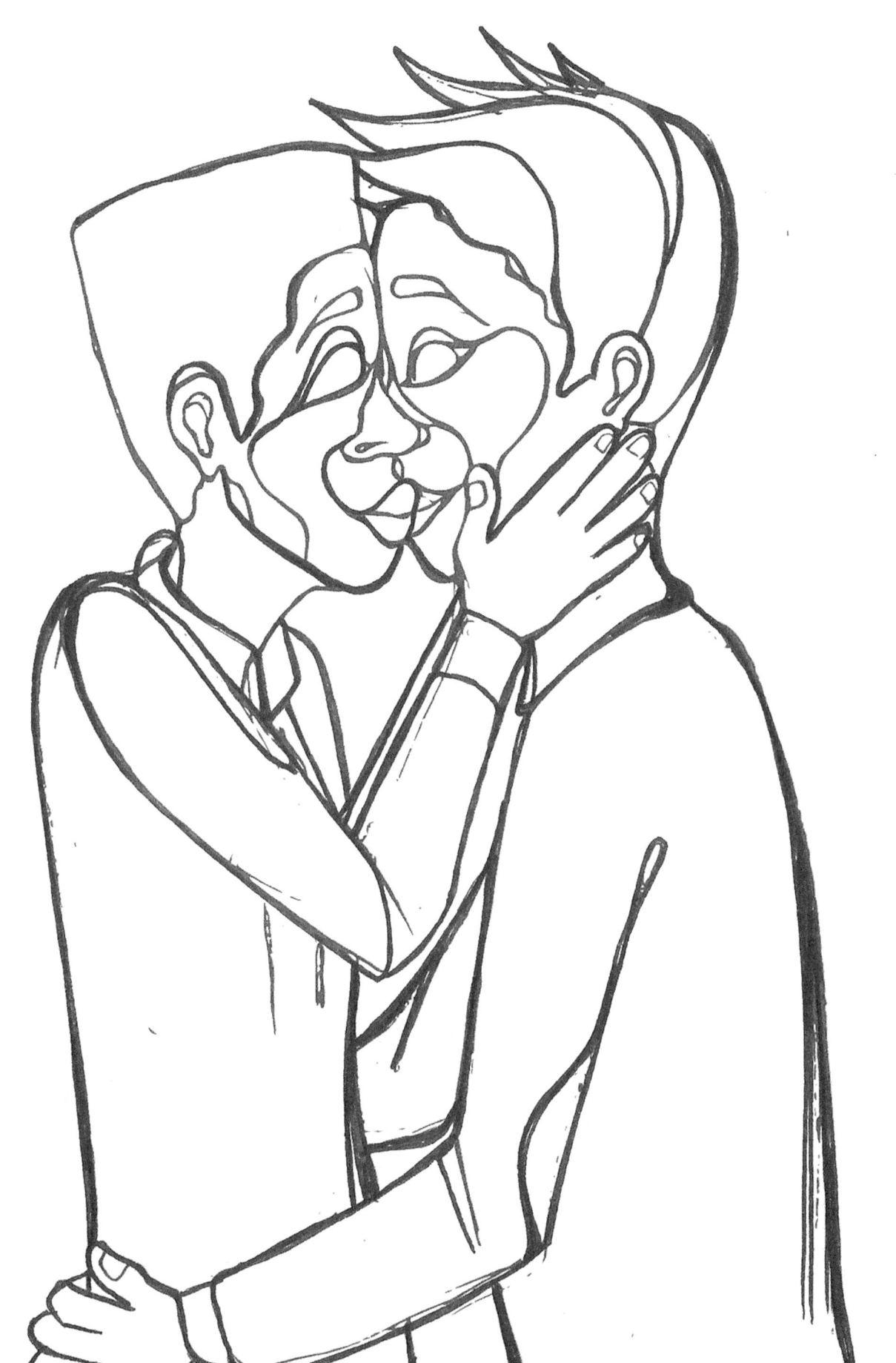

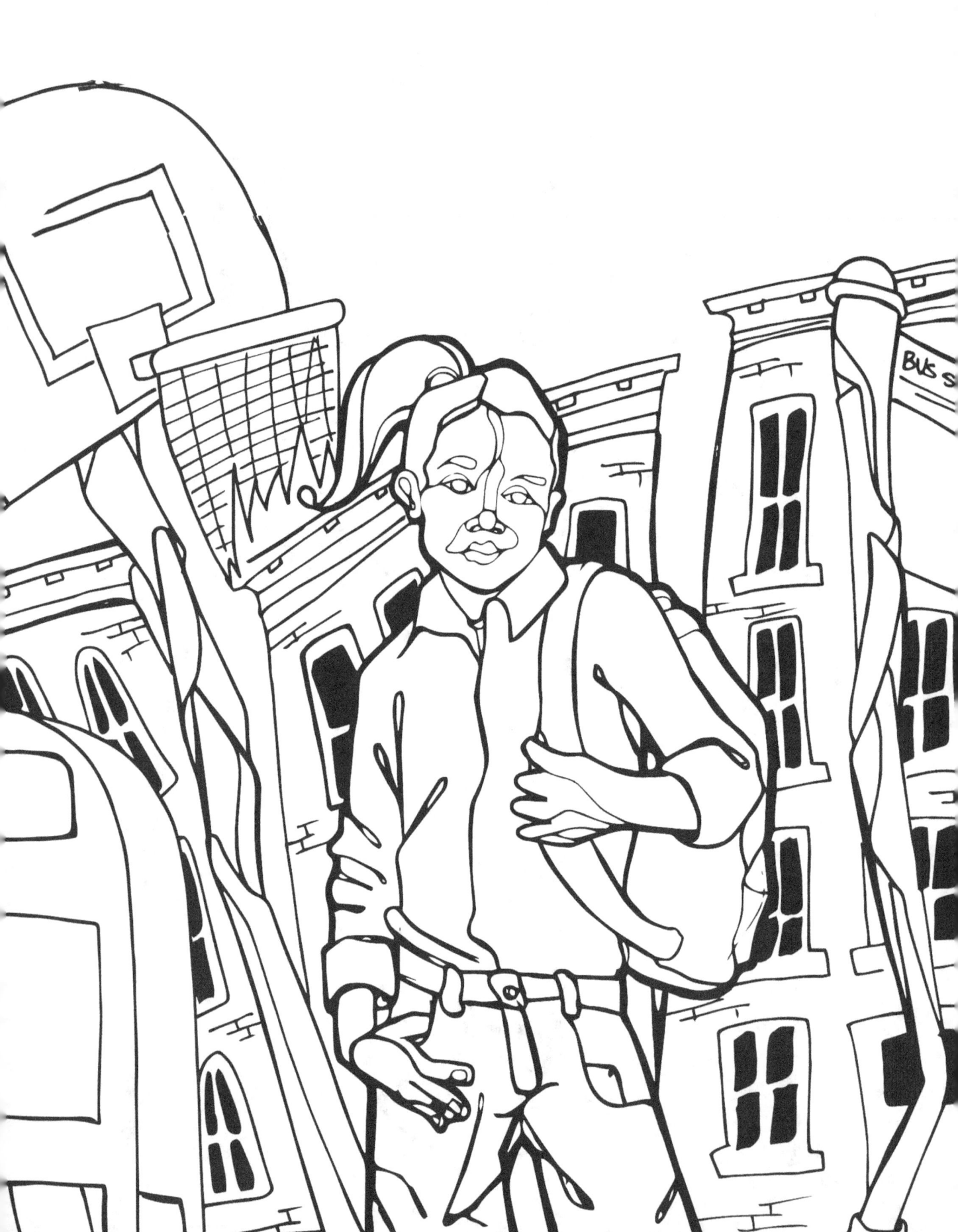

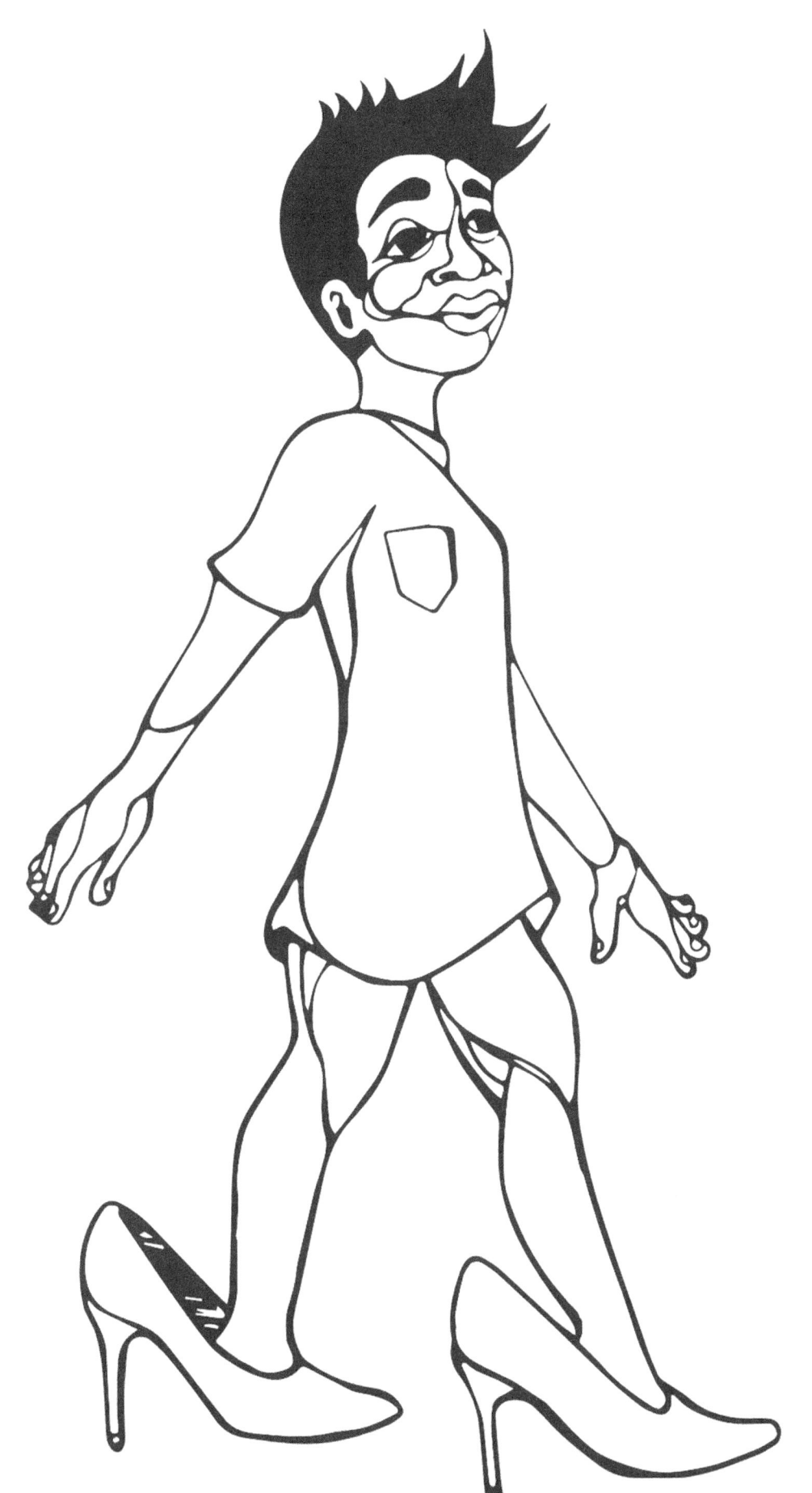

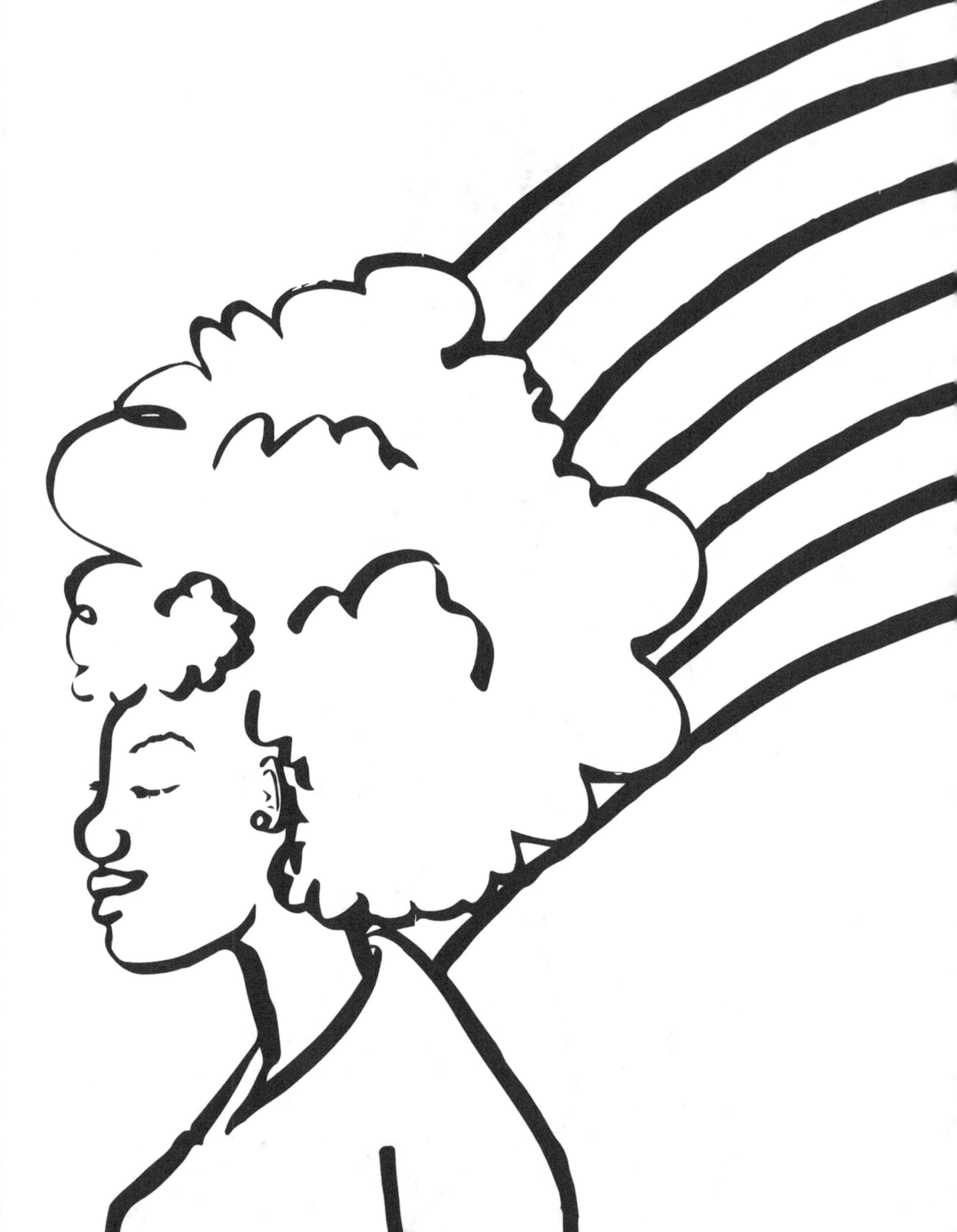

BE WHO YOU ARE.

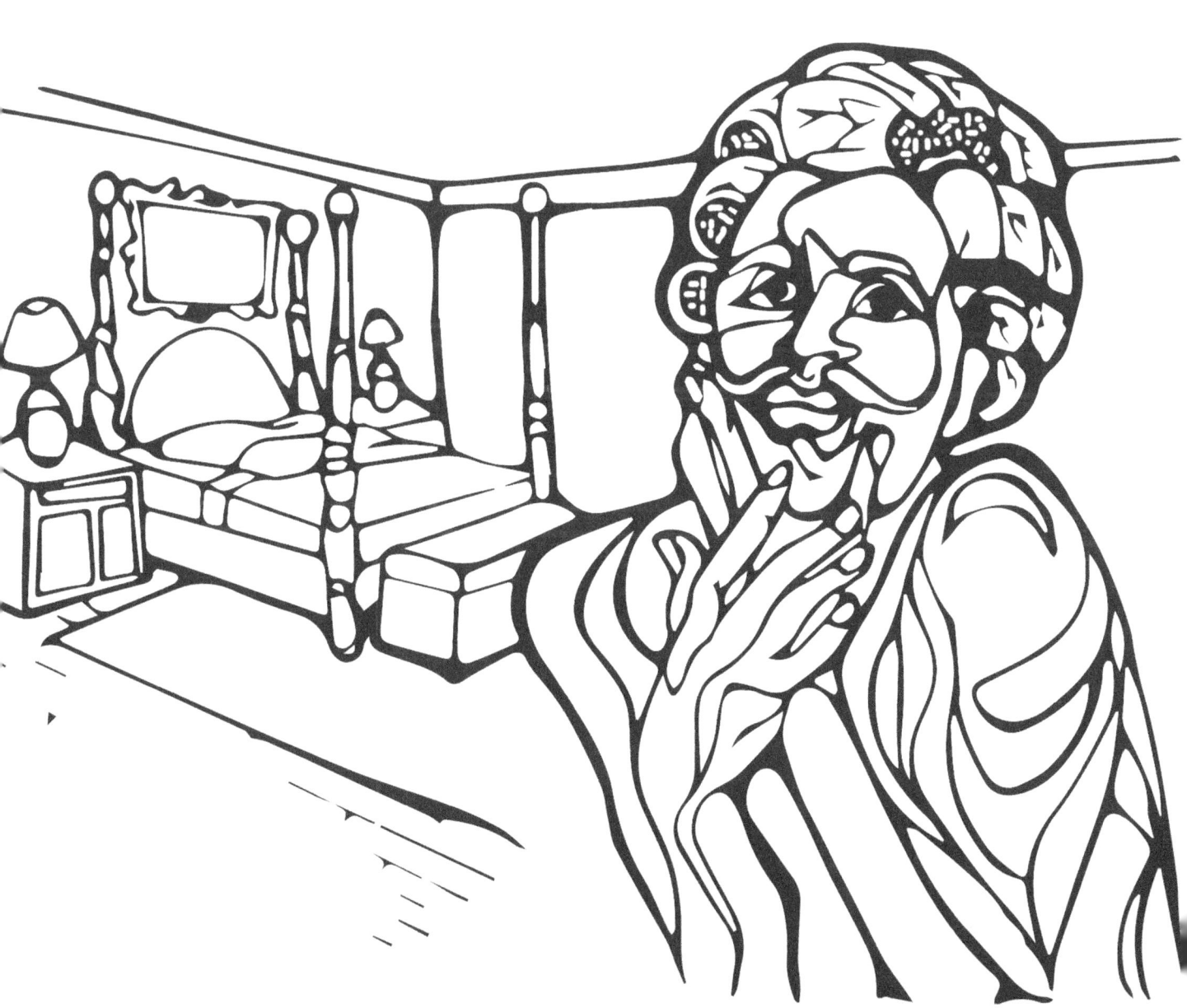

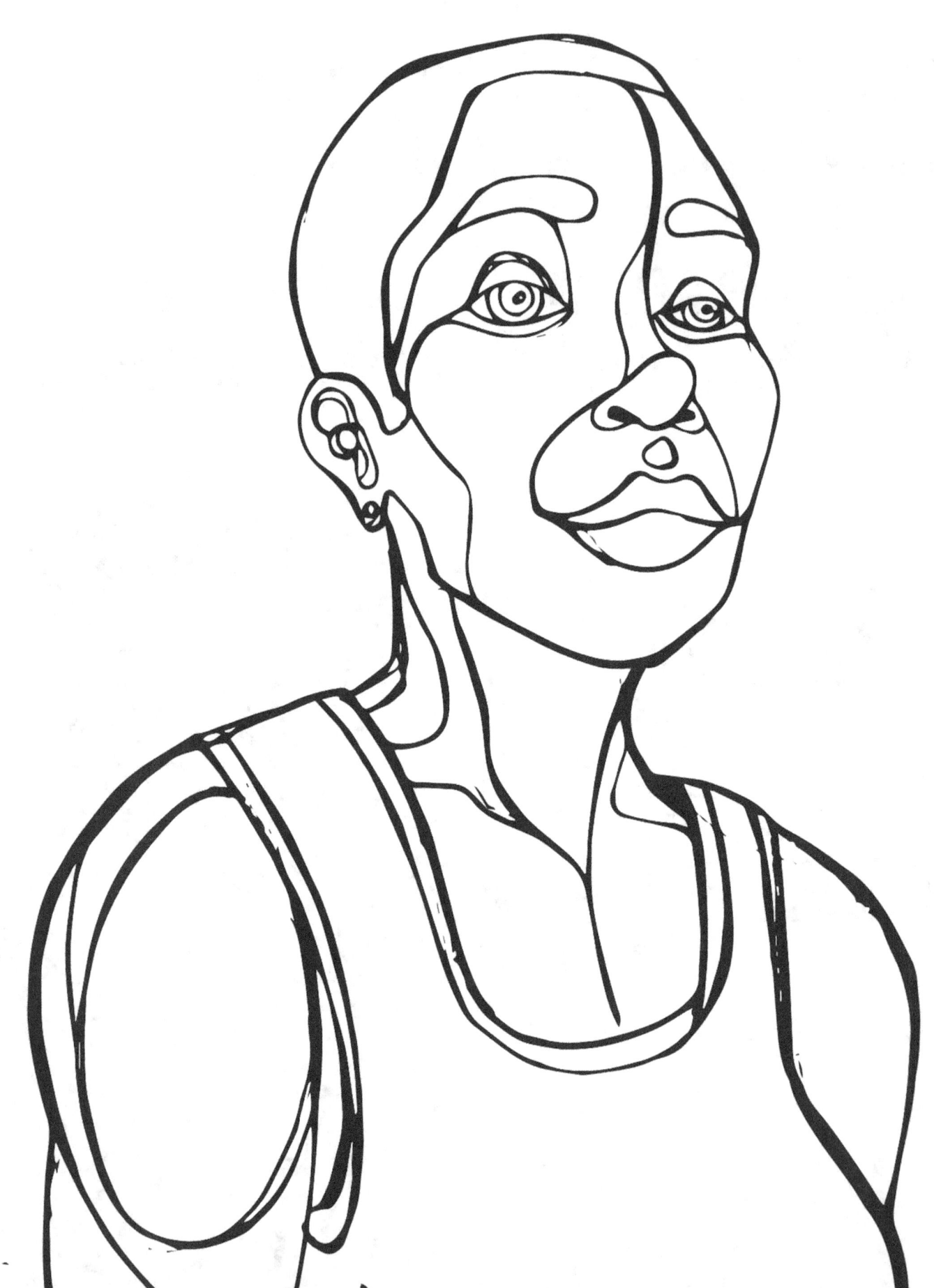

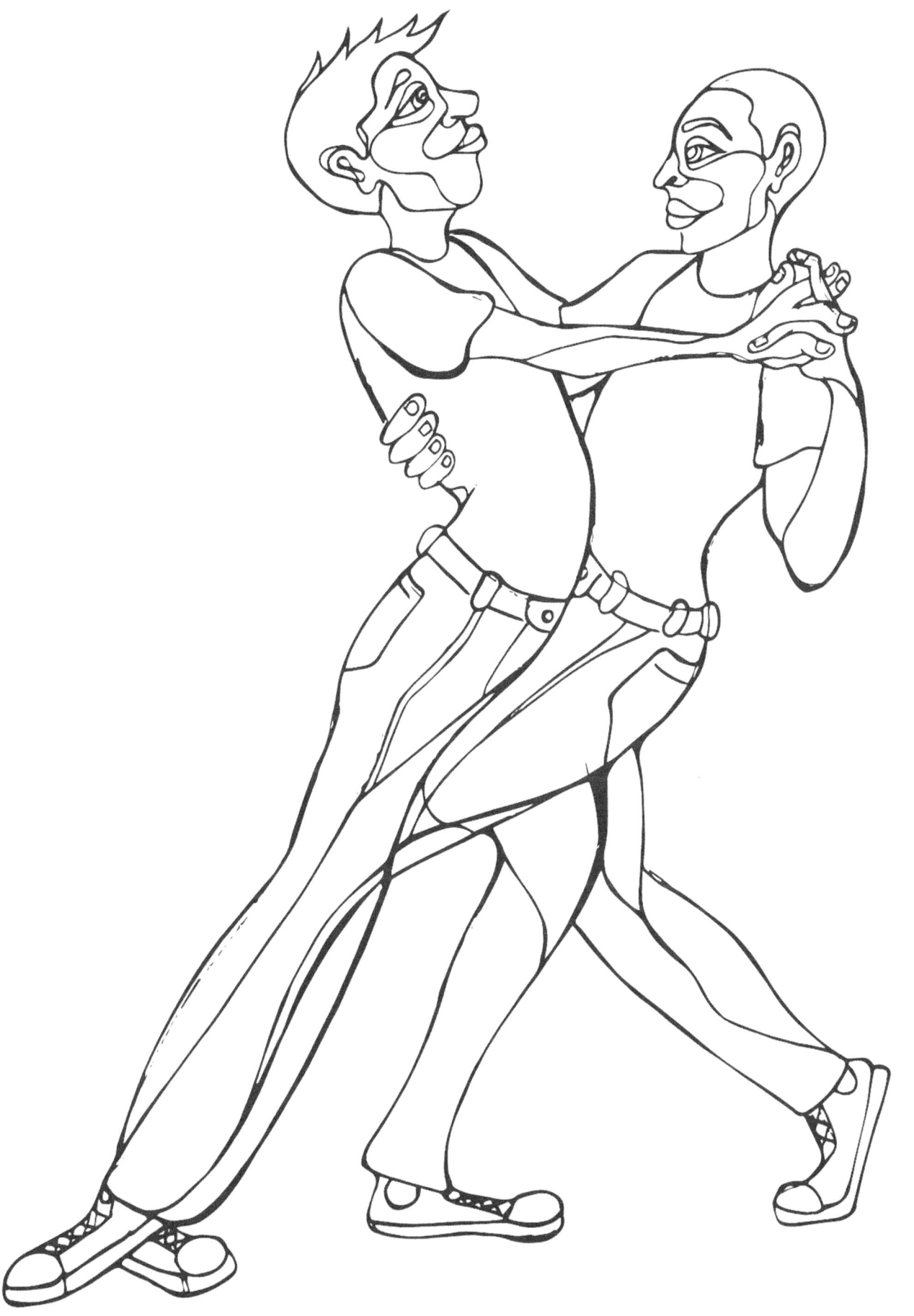

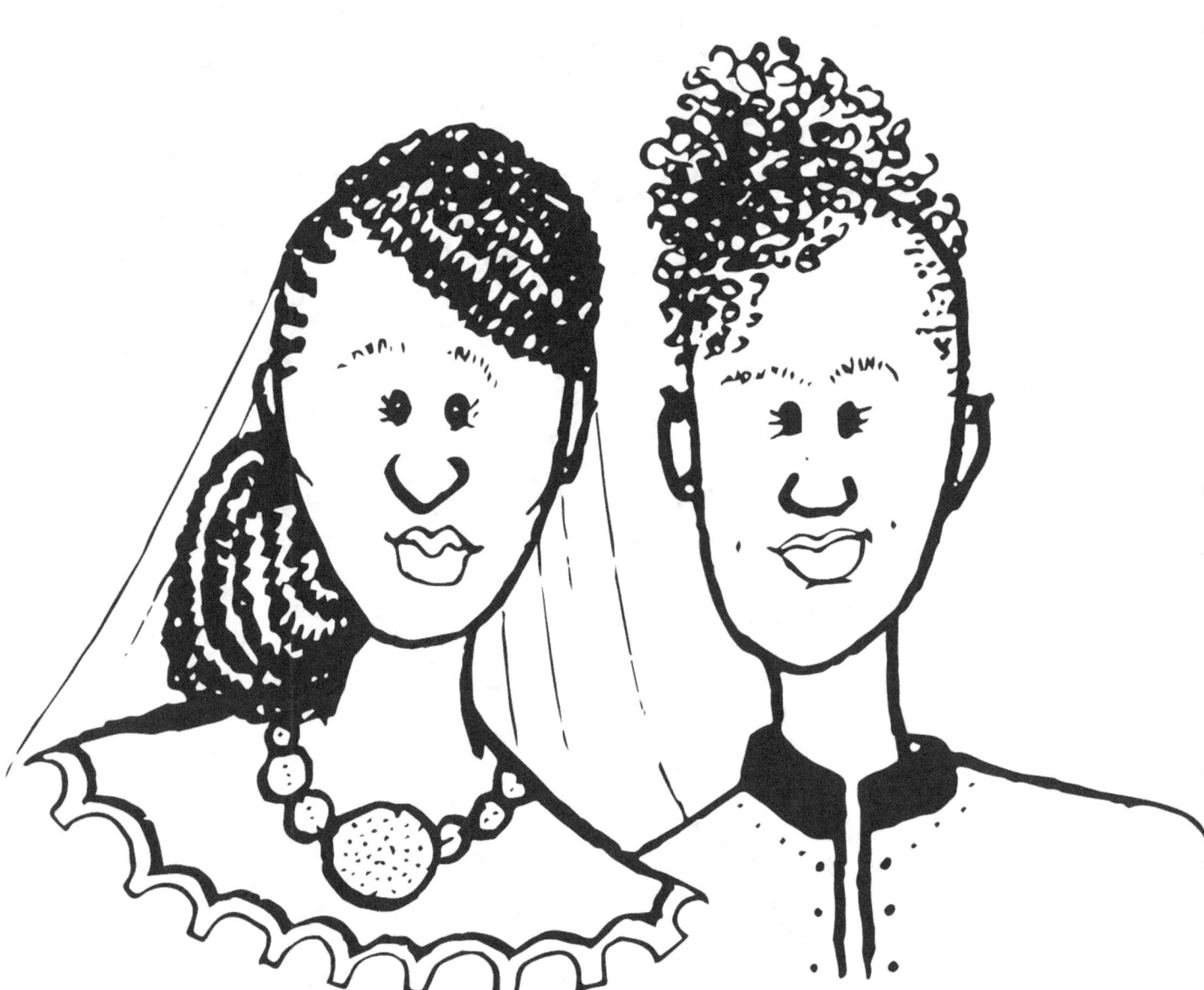

{about the illustrators}

Sam Kirk creates artwork to celebrate people and to inspire pride and recognition for underrepresented communities. Her work walks the viewer through various memories focusing on celebration of culture, discovery of identity, and the politics that we have been fighting for generations. Born and raised on the south side of Chicago, working class communities are a key ingredient of inspiration in her continual study to share her appreciation of everyday people. Part autobiographical, and part fairytale, her vibrant color palette reveals profound stories laced with optimism. To learn more about her work visit iamsamkirk.com.

sam kirk

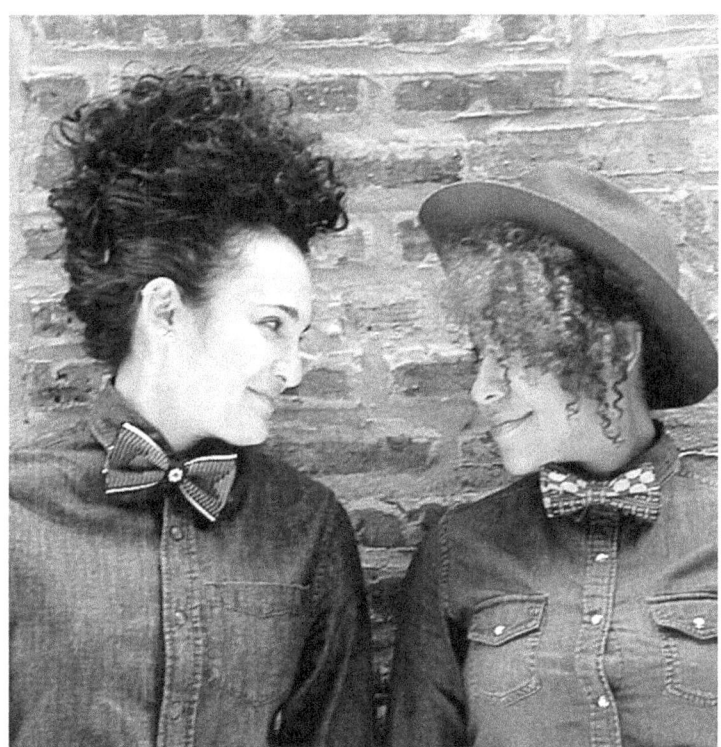

jenny Q.

Adventures of a girl born in Brooklyn, a.k.a. Jenny Cunningham shares her experiences from her travels across the globe. A professional cultural dancer of various genres for more than a decade, Jenny was recently injured leaving her with months of recovery. During this time she rekindled her love for drawing. She is currently working on a new graphic novel, Quirklyn ™. While the full comic series is in the works, she continues to pursue magic throughout her "fun-sized adventures." To learn more about Jenny visit, JennyRaQs.com for dance info and Quirklyn.com for her upcoming comic series.

stay in the know

@iamsamkirk
@quirklyn

buy more things made by us at
provokeculture.com